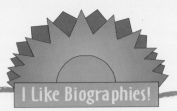

I Like Biographies!

Read About
Sacagawea

Stephen Feinstein

Enslow Publishers, Inc.

40 Industrial Road   PO Box 38
Box 398   Aldershot
Berkeley Heights, NJ 07922   Hants GU12 6BP
USA   UK

http://www.enslow.com

Words to Know

explorer—A person who travels into new lands.

Minnetaree (Mih-neh-TA-ree)—An Indian tribe that lived along the Missouri River in North Dakota.

moccasin—A soft slipper made of leather.

Shoshone (Sho-SHO-nee)—An Indian tribe that lived on both sides of the Rocky Mountains.

Library of Congress Cataloging-in-Publication Data

Feinstein, Stephen.
　　Read about Sacagawea / Stephen Feinstein.
　　　p. cm. — (I like biographies!)
　　Includes bibliographical references and index.
　　ISBN 0-7660-2297-8
　　1. Sacagawea—Juvenile literature. 2. Shoshoni women—Biography—Juvenile literature. 3. Shoshoni Indians—Biography—Juvenile literature. 4. Lewis and Clark Expedition (1804–1806)—Juvenile literature. [1. Sacagawea. 2. Shoshoni Indians—Biography. 3. Indians of North America—Biography. 4. Women—Biography. 5. Lewis and Clark Expedition (1804–1806)] I. Title. II. Series.
　　F592.7.S123F45 2004
　　978.004'974574'0092--dc22
　　　　　　　[B]
　　　　　　　　　　　　2003024395

Printed in the United States of America

10 9 8 7 6 5 4 3 2 1

To Our Readers: We have done our best to make sure all Internet Addresses in this book were active and appropriate when we went to press. However, the author and the publisher have no control over and assume no liability for the material available on those Internet sites or on links to other Web sites. Any comments or suggestions can be sent by e-mail to comments@enslow.com or to the address on the back cover.

Illustration Credits: AP/Wide World, p. 21; © Artville, LLC, p. 11; Denver Public Library, Western History Collection, call no. X-33784, p. 1; Drawing by George Henry in *Sacajawea*, by Harold P. Howard. Published by the University of Oklahoma Press, Norman, 1971, p. 17; Library of Congress, p. 5; Edgar S. Paxson, "Sacagawea," oil on canvas, 1904, permanent collection The Montana Museum of Art and Culture, The University of Montana, p. 7; Courtesy Frederic Remington Art Museum, Ogdensburg, New York, p. 19; Charles M. Russell, "Lewis and Clark on the Lower Columbia," 1905, watercolor, 1961.195, © Amon Carter Museum, Fort Worth, Tex., p. 13; Charles M. Russell, "Lewis and Clark Expedition." From the collection of the Gilcrease Museum, Tulsa, Okla., p. 15; State Historical Society of North Dakota 85.22, p. 9; United States Mint, p. 3.

Cover Illustration: Painting by Carl Feryok.

Contents

Chapter 1

Growing Up in an Indian Village

Sacagawea was born in 1788. Her tribe of Shoshone Indians lived in the Rocky Mountains. When she was eleven, Sacagawea was captured by the Minnetaree Indians during a raid. They took Sacagawea to their village far to the east on the Great Plains.

The Shoshone lived in tepees like these.

5

Sacagawea grew into a strong young woman. She worked hard, helping the Minnetaree women grow corn, beans, and squash. The Minnetaree called her Bird Woman, a sign of respect. Sacagawea wished that she could fly like a bird. Then she would be able to fly home.

There are no photographs of Sacagawea. This is what one artist thought she might have looked like.

In 1804, Sacagawea was sixteen. She was now married to a French Canadian fur trapper named Toussaint Charbonneau. One day, a group of forty white men traveled up the Missouri River in three boats. They were led by the explorers Meriwether Lewis and William Clark.

This shows the first meeting between the explorers and Sacagawea. Behind them are the round earth houses of the Minnetaree.

They had been sent by President Thomas Jefferson to explore the lands west of the Missouri River. They were looking for somebody who could speak to the Indians they would meet. They asked Sacagawea to come along to speak with the Shoshone. She could hardly believe her good luck! She would finally be going home.

This map shows the route that the explorers took across America, from St. Louis to the Pacific Ocean.

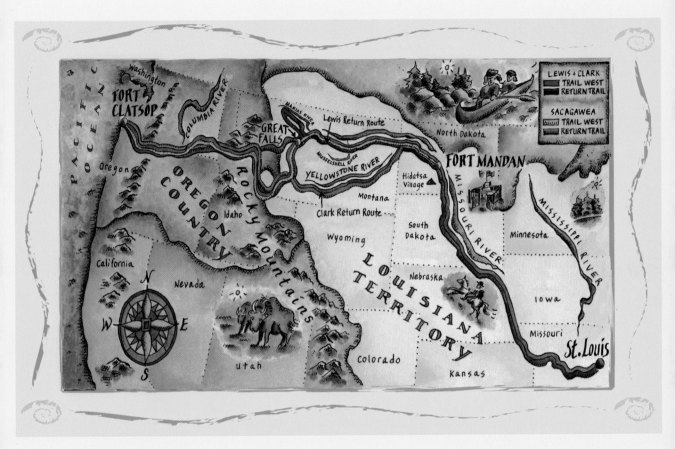

In April 1805, Lewis and Clark and their men set out across the plains. Charbonneau and Sacagawea walked with them. Sacagawea carried her two-month-old son Pomp on her back.

Sacagawea helped find food for the group. She gathered wood for the campfire. She even made moccasins for the men.

Sacagawea helped Lewis and Clark in many ways. She spoke with other Indians and told them the explorers were friendly.

After traveling through the Rocky Mountains, the explorers met a group of Shoshone Indians. Suddenly Sacagawea's eyes filled with tears of happiness. One of the Indians was her brother Cameauhwait! She had not seen him since they were children. Now he was a chief. Sacagawea threw her arms around him.

Sacagawea was very happy when they met the Shoshone. In this painting, she is hugging a friend from her childhood.

Chapter 4

Sacagawea Sees the "Great Waters"

Sacagawea knew that Lewis and Clark wanted to go all the way to the "great waters." This was her name for the Pacific Ocean. Sacagawea hoped to see the "great waters" too. Her brother said he would help the explorers. He gave them horses for the trip.

Sacagawea helped the explorers get horses from the Shoshone. Here she is riding with Pomp on her back.

16

Once again the group traveled west. When they reached the Columbia River, they built canoes. They then traveled down the Columbia all the way to the Pacific Ocean. On November 15, 1805, Sacagawea stood on the beach. She could not take her eyes off the huge waves of the "great waters."

This painting shows Lewis and Clark with Sacagawea and Charbonneau standing behind them. They are all in front of the Columbia River, which leads to the Pacific Ocean.

Sacagawea spent the winter on the beach with the explorers. She then traveled with them back to the Indian village on the Missouri River.

The brave Bird Woman died in December 1812. Lewis and Clark could not have made their trip without the help of Sacagawea.

There are many statues honoring Sacagawea. This one is in Portland, Oregon.

Timeline

1788—Sacagawea is born to the Shoshone tribe.

About 1798—Sacagawea is captured by the Minnetaree Indians.

1804—Lewis and Clark begin their trip to explore the lands west of the Missouri River. Sacagawea joins them.

February 1805—Pomp is born.

August 1805—Sacagawea meets the Shoshone Indians again.

November 1805—The explorers reach the Pacific Ocean.

1806—The explorers travel back east. Sacagawea returns to the Minnetaree.

1812—Sacagawea dies in South Dakota.

Learn More

Books

Adler, David A. *A Picture Book of Sacagawea*. New York: Holiday House, 2000.

Devillier, Christy. *Lewis & Clark*. Edina, Minn.: Abdo Publishing, 2001.

Milton, Joyce. *Sacajawea: Her True Story*. New York: Grosset & Dunlap, 2001.

Redmond, Shirley-Raye. *Lewis and Clark: A Prairie Dog for the President*. New York: Random House, 2003.

Internet Addresses

Lewis and Clark Journey of Discovery

<http://www.nps.gov/jeff/LewisClark2/HomePage/HomePage.htm>

National Geographic Kids, "Go West Across America with Lewis & Clark"

<http://nationalgeographic.com/west>

Index